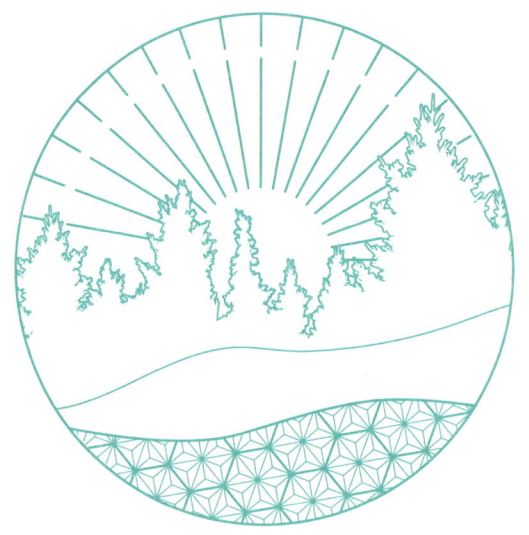

INSIGHTS

an imprint of

INSIGHT EDITIONS

www.insighteditions.com

Copyright © 2021 Insight Editions.
All rights reserved.

MANUFACTURED IN CHINA

10 9 8 7 6 5 4 3 2 1

INSIGHTS

an imprint of

INSIGHT EDITIONS

www.insighteditions.com

Copyright © 2021 Insight Editions.
All rights reserved.

MANUFACTURED IN CHINA

10 9 8 7 6 5 4 3 2 1

INSIGHTS
an imprint of
INSIGHT EDITIONS
www.insighteditions.com

Copyright © 2021 Insight Editions.
All rights reserved.

MANUFACTURED IN CHINA
10 9 8 7 6 5 4 3 2 1